DRUGS the facts about
ALCOHOL

DRUGS the facts about
ALCOHOL

TED GOTTFRIED

BENCHMARK BOOKS

MARSHALL CAVENDISH
NEW YORK

For Sweet Loraine

Acknowledgments
I am grateful to personnel of the Humanities and Social Sciences
Library and the Mid-Manhattan Library of the New York Public
Library, the Queens Borough Public Library, Alcoholics
Anonymous, Drinkwatchers, Advocates for Recovery, and many
others for aid in gathering material for this book. Also, gratitude
and much love to my wife, Harriet Gottfried, who, as always, read
and critiqued the manuscript. Her help was invaluable, but any
shortcomings in the work are mine alone.

Benchmark Books
Marshall Cavendish
99 White Plains Road
Tarrytown, NY 10591-9001
www.marshallcavendish.com

Text copyright © 2005 by Marshall Cavendish Corporation
Illustrations copyright © 2005 by Marshall Cavendish Corporation

Library of Congress Cataloging-in-Publication Data
Gottfried, Ted.
The facts about alcohol / by Ted Gottfried.
p. cm. – (Drugs)
Includes bibliographical references and index.
ISBN 0-7614-1805-9
1. Drinking of alcoholic beverages–United States–Juvenile literature. 2.
Alcoholism–United States–Juvenile literature. 3. Youth–Alcohol use–United
States–Juvenile literature. I. Title. II. Series: Drugs (Benchmark Books (Firm))

HV5066.G68 2004
362.292'0973–dc22
2004005388

Photo research by Joan Meisel
Cover photo: Royalty Free/Corbis
Corbis: Owen Franken, 24; Wally McNamee, 48; AFP, 50; Richard Hutchings, 53;
Royalty-Free, 64. *Hulton Archive by Getty Images:* 16, 28, 37, 38, 42, 45. *North Wind
Picture Archives:* 12, 33.

Series design by Sonia Chaghatzbanian

Printed in China
1 3 5 6 4 2

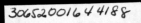

CONTENTS

> ... The night they invented Champagne,
> They absolutely knew,
> That all we'd want to do
> Is fly to the sky on Champagne ...
>
> —Song by Alan Jay Lerner, from the film *Gigi*

Preface

Alcohol—champagne, beer, wine, whiskey, liquor of all kinds—can be a trip. Sometimes it's a fun trip. Sometimes it's a distressing trip. Sometimes it's a tragic trip. And sometimes it's a fatal trip. Too many times the fun trip becomes distressing, leads to tragedy, causes death. Sometimes this happens, but not always, and that's why the problem arises. A drink can make you feel good; two drinks, better; three, still better (or maybe not, maybe sick). But at some point, the body reacts.

The two major effects of alcohol are stimulation and depression. In the short term the drinker is exhilarated and feels good. In the long term—the morning after a party or the weeks following a binge—he or she is brought down, feels dejected, sinks into inertia or despair, and may become suicidal. Reactions vary from person to person. They are determined not so much by what a person drinks as by the amount of alcohol consumed and a variety of other factors. These include age, sex, body weight, heredity, physical condition, psychological mood, and other outside circumstances.

Did You Know That:

- 100,000 people die each year from alcohol abuse?

- Alcohol abuse (especially high-risk drinking) is becoming a major problem on college campuses?

- The direct and indirect costs of alcoholism—lost productivity, absenteeism, medical claims, and accidents—are in excess of $140 billion each year?

- A recent national study shows that 82 percent of doctors admit that members of their profession avoid dealing with alcoholism in their patients, 60 percent of employers avoid addressing alcoholism in the workforce, and 60 percent of clergymen side-step confronting members of their congregation suffering from alcoholism?

- Every dollar spent on alcoholism treatment will save four to seven dollars?

Source: American Council on Alcoholism

While some groups may be more at risk for serious consequences from drinking alcohol than others, the majority of people who drink may suffer no worse results than an occasional hangover. As of the year 2000, the U.S. census put the population of the United States at 281 million people. According to a May 2002 Gallup Poll, 64 percent of Americans have occasion to use alcoholic beverages, such as scotch, wine, or beer. In other words, the majority of Americans take an occasional drink. "Responsible consumption of distilled spirits, beer, or wine is part of a normal, healthy adult lifestyle," according to David Holliday, vice president of the Distilled Spirits Council of the United States (DISCUS).

On the other hand, according to the American Council on Alcoholism, over 20 million people throughout the United States (an estimated 10 percent of the population) have a serious problem with alcohol. Often a problem drinker will affect six other people. This represents over 120 million people—of all ages, socioeconomic levels, races, and creeds, a number approaching half of the U.S. population.

The statistics on drinking can be confusing. There is a tendency to use them either to attack alcohol consumption or to support the view that a couple of drinks won't hurt a person. It's an issue that many young adults face often. There is a party. Everybody is relaxed and having a good time. Beer, wine, or hard liquor is served. Everybody has a drink, gulps a drink, sips a drink, or simply holds an alcoholic beverage in their hand. The peer pressure may not be heavy-handed. It may be unspoken, subtle, but it probably exists.

Should you have a drink? Will one drink lower your resistance to having a second drink? Will you have more drinks at the next party, next weekend? Will you have a drink between parties? More than one? Are you on your way to having a drinking problem or to becoming an alcoholic?

The answers to such questions are not carved in stone. The first drink doesn't have to lead to a second one. Lips that touch liquor don't necessarily drown in it. One drink is not the first step on the road to perdition. That said, it still must be noted that alcohol poses more of a danger to young people than to older population groups.

For one thing, the younger a person starts to drink, the more likely he or she is to develop a serious drinking problem, with the probability of it evolving into alcoholism. According to a series of studies evaluated by Enoch Gordis, director of the National Institute on Alcohol Abuse and Alcoholism (NIAAA), about 40 percent of those who begin drinking before age fifteen and 25 percent of those who begin drinking at age seventeen are at risk of establishing a damaging habit of alcohol abuse that will be hard to break. By contrast, only 10 percent of those who first try alcohol at ages twenty-one or twenty-two are at risk.

Young adults and alcohol are a combination that may have other dangerous consequences. There is an established link between the high suicide rate of twelve-to eighteen-year-olds (the highest of any age group in the country) and alcohol consumption. Alcohol may not be a cause of suicide, but it can deepen depression and lower resistance to self-destructive impulses.

Binge drinking (guzzling beer or hard liquor to the point of passing out) among high school and college students has resulted in illness, expulsion, unwanted pregnancies, date rapes, and death. School failure and dropout rates are often the result of an ongoing pattern of alcohol consumption. In general, young people have more car accidents and cause a greater number of serious injuries and deaths due to driving while drunk than drivers over age twenty-fve. All states and most cities have laws against drinking and driving, and the penalties can be severe.

There are also laws against minors drinking, with punishments ranging from separation from one's family to incarceration or fines. Most importantly, people under the age of eighteen are still developing mentally, physically, and emotionally, and the rate of development is different for each individual. Decision-making ability will vary from one young person to another.

The truth about drinking is elusive. Alcohol is a neutral substance, neither bad nor good in itself. It is how people use it, or abuse it, that makes it bad or good. Young adults will be faced with making decisions about drinking. The purpose of this book is to provide the facts to help them make these decisions that can affect their whole lives.

Fermented wines were indulged in freely at Roman banquets. The prevalence of liquor, particularly among aristocrats, contributed to the rapid decline and eventual collapse of the Roman Empire.

At the punch-bowl's brink,
Let the thirsty think,
What they say in Japan:
First the man takes a drink,
Then the drink takes a drink,
Then the drink takes the man!

—"An Adage from the Orient,"
by Edward Rowland Sill (1841-1887)

1 What's in a Drink?

Among the alcoholic beverages discussed through-
out this book are wine, beer, spirits (scotch and rye
whiskies, bourbon, gin, vodka, brandy, rum), and
liqueurs (variously flavored hard liquors). These can
be swigged from a bottle, gulped from a shot glass,
guzzled from a can, ladled from a punch bowl, or
sipped from a champagne goblet. Liquor can pick
you up, or lay you down. Liquor makes the world go
round—or makes it stop.

The Accidental High

It began as an accident more than ten thousand
years ago. A bunch of grapes—or honey, or berries,
or other fruit, or a combination of such ingredi-
ents—was warmed enough for fermentation to

occur. Fermentation happens when yeasts convert natural sugar to alcohol and carbon dioxide. Early human beings tasted the fermented product, found it to their taste, and drank enough to discover that it had a pleasant effect—or at least so it seemed. They may not have connected those first binges with the morning-after hangovers that followed them. In any case, they were soon deliberately fermenting various products and storing the syrups and juices in earthen jars or wooden casks. Fermented drinks had become a part of humankind's life on Earth.

It happened the same way, at different times, in many parts of the world. Local climate and agricultural conditions determined just what kind of liquor early societies developed. In ancient Persia the juice of fermented grapes was drunk from pottery jugs. Grape wine was also the drink of choice in the Egypt of the pharaohs and in early Greece. Throughout the Mediterranean region wine was also made from other varieties of fruit. Fig, pomegranate, and date wines were popular. Ancient peoples made liquor from red algae in Siberia, maple syrup in North America, cactus in Central America, palm stems in South Africa, and rice in China and Japan.

Beer was developed during the same prehistoric period as wine. Wheat and barley were soaked in water to make gruel. The potion was left out in the air to ferment. According to available records, the ancient Egyptians made beer from a type of wheat known as emmer even before they developed the skill to bake bread. Today, barley beer is still made in the same way. The ancient Egyptian goddess of beer, Menquet, was pictured on tablets balancing two jugs. Hathor, the goddess of the grapevine, was depicted as a sacred cow and was paid homage once a month on a "Day of Intoxication."

Beastly Drunks

Liquor, or distilled spirits—the so-called hard stuff sold in liquor stores—such as whiskey, gin, and vodka developed in early civilizations in every part of the world. By 800 B.C.E. the Chinese were distilling a beverage from rice beer. Mead, a particularly strong alcoholic beverage, was made from fermented honey. Before 1000 C.E., Arab tribes were distilling strong liquor from wine, as were the Greeks and Romans, while the British were making whiskey from grain. Arab invaders introduced distillation techniques to western Europe, while in eastern Europe potatoes were fermented and processed for vodka.

The distilling process is relatively simple. A substance that has fermented—its natural sugar has been transformed into alcohol—is heated to a point above 173.3 degrees Fahrenheit (78.5 degrees Celsius) but below 212 °F (100 °C). This causes the alcohol to vaporize and separate from the original substance. The vapor is then gathered and recondensed into a liquid of much greater alcoholic strength.

As people began drinking the hard stuff, drunkenness became a problem in virtually every society.

IN THE MIDDLE AGES, WINE WAS MADE BY TREADING BAREFOOT ON THE GRAPES
(A CUSTOM THAT PREVAILS IN SOME VINEYARDS TODAY). BACK THEN IT WAS THE
PEASANTS WHO HARVESTED THE GRAPES AND STOMPED ON THEM. SOMETIMES,
HOWEVER, THEY LOOKED LIKE THEY WERE HAVING SO MUCH FUN JUMPING UP
AND DOWN THAT NOBLES, AS SHOWN HERE, TOOK OVER THE GRAPE STOMPING.

The types of behavior people displayed when drunk were described as animal antics by the sixteenth century English writer Thomas Nashe. An ape drunk, he asserted, was someone who jumped, yelled, and chattered like a monkey. A lion drunk roared and fought. A fox drunk was sly and sneaky; a swine drunk, sodden and lethargic; a sheep drunk, robbed of coherence and able only to bleat. A goat drunk, particularly scorned by Nashe, ". . . hath no minde but on Lecherie."

Bugs and Baboons

In fact, animals actually do get drunk. In the year 1545 insect drunkenness led to an impromptu trial. Strange and mystical evidence was presented both for and against local insects by the wine growers of St. Julien, France. After imbibing grapes that had been fermented by the heat, the bugs had destroyed the area's vineyards. Records were kept of the trial, which involved a prosecutor who argued that the insects were subject to the laws of the land, and a defense attorney who pleaded that they were only pursuing the biblical order to be fruitful (that is, by consuming grapes) and multiply. Sadly, the last page of the trial record, which contained the judge's decision, is missing. It was eaten by weevils.

Some people who keep carrier pigeons use grain soaked in alcohol to train them to return to the coop. They lie around in a stupor until their next mission, but they always come back for another binge. Some owners of parrots feed them fermented fruits or small quantities of distilled liquor to make them more talkative. Starlings also are attracted to certain wines and other kinds of alcohol. They are one of the few animals—including man, in many cases—capable of regulating their drinking enough to get high without getting sick or passing out.

Raccoons can also control their drinking. When they raid campers' tents, they head straight for the beer or whiskey bottles and have learned to pull out the corks or unscrew the caps for themselves. They guzzle away but always stop before they get drunk. Most other animals don't exercise such control.

A herd of 150 elephants in West Bengal stampeded after drinking liquor in a distillery. Five people were killed and a dozen more were injured in the rampage, which destroyed twenty village shanties and seven concrete buildings. Closer to home, squirrels seek out fermented sap on trees, get high, and bounce around like crazed pinballs, frequently missing the mark when they jump from one branch to another and plummeting to the ground. Bears and foxes also seek out intoxicating saps and syrups from trees and plants. In warmer climates from South America to the Sudan, wild animals such as cougars, lions, and monkeys lap up the fermented ooze from rotting fruit and become inebriated. Sometimes monkeys fall on the fruit in groups and have what can only be described as a party.

Beasts, like humans, can suffer beastly hangovers. The scientist Charles Darwin wrote about wild baboons trapped with bowls of beer by natives in northeastern Africa. The animals would consume as much of the beer as they could and fall into drunken stupors. When they awoke the next morning, they were ". . . very cross and dismal; they held their aching heads with both hands, and wore a pitiable expression; when beer was offered them, they turned away with disgust."

Alcohol and the Body

The effects of alcohol on animals are pretty much the same as the effects on humans. When an alcoholic beverage is consumed, it is diluted by the stomach juices and quickly distributed throughout the body. Must of it is absorbed into the bloodstream before it is digested. The alcohol passes to the small intestine, where it is quickly absorbed and circulated. The rate of absorption varies according to what kind of alcoholic beverage has been drunk and how much food is in the stomach. Fatty foods in particular delay absorption. Liquor mixed with carbonated soda is absorbed more rapidly. Cocktails made by mixing different kinds of liquor, or liquor and wine, are also absorbed more quickly. Absorbed alcohol is diluted by the body's natural fluids. When quickly absorbed, intoxication occurs promptly.

Understanding Alcohol

According to the American Dietetic Association:

• A standard serving of beer, distilled spirits, or wine each contains the same amount of alcohol, approximately 25 grams of pure ethanol (the ethyl alcohol present in all such beverages). Knowing the facts of beverage alcohol equivalency is a critical aspect of responsible drinking.

• According to the federal Dietary Guidelines for Americans, moderation is defined as consuming no more than one drink per day for women and no more than two drinks per day for men. The limits are based on differences between the sexes in both weight and metabolism. The following count as a drink:

   12 ounces of regular beer (150 calories)
   5 ounces of wine (100 calories)
   1.5 ounces of 80-proof distilled spirits (100 calories)

Surprisingly, most adults do not understand the facts of beverage alcohol equivalency. For example, a recent national survey of adults 21 and older found that 46 percent of adults surveyed knew that a mixed drink made with 1.5 ounces of 80-proof distilled spirits, 12 ounces of beer, and 5 ounces of wine all contain the same amount of alcohol.

There are several immediate and short-term effects of intoxication. These vary from person to person because of many factors, the most common of which is body chemistry, or metabolism. In general, the effects may include dizziness, disorientation, nausea, and either exhilaration or weariness, or one leading into the other.

Both the brain and the central nervous system are affected. Inhibitions are lowered, ordinary restraints on behavior are relaxed, and judgment is affected. Since alcohol is chemically classified as a depressant, the initial jolt of excitement that a drink can provide will ultimately fade away and a sort of dejection will usually replace it. The usual progression leads to a state of both mental and physical weariness.

A Grim Picture

The adverse effects of drunkenness are made worse by follow-up drinks and by the shortness of the time between drinks. Unwelcome results, such as throwing up, passing out, becoming sexually bold or belligerent, occur when drinks are gulped rather than sipped or when the drinks are not spaced out, but swallowed one after the other. More dangerous are repeated drinking bouts over short periods of time in which the body becomes accustomed to the initial uplift the liquor provides, and the drinker responds by increasing the intake.

People who follow this course are either well on their way to becoming alcoholics or have already reached this stage. Frequent heavy drinking can harm many of the body's organs. Overuse of alcohol damages the tissues of the mouth, esophagus, and stomach. Cirrhosis is common among alcoholics. Many suffer from polyneuropathy—a degenerative disease of the nervous system that affects both reflexes and judgment. *Delirium tremens* (commonly known as D.T.'s), a combination of a lack of motor control and hallucinations usually accompanied by exaggerated fears, occur during withdrawal from alcohol. Many psychological problems are an integral part of alcoholism. Many of the physical conditions can be fatal. The World Health Organization estimates that alcohol causes more death and disability than tobacco or illegal drugs do.

This is a grim picture, but it has another side. Many social drinkers—those who have one or two drinks a day—are not alcoholics. As far back as 1979, the role of red wine in lowering coronary artery disease was confirmed by researchers. Countries like France and Italy, where wine with meals was part of the culture, had (and still have) much lower rates of heart attacks than nations like Finland, Scotland, and the United States, where people consumed far less wine. This was surprising because the French eat much more butter, cheese, liver, and other foods high in animal fats, which clog the arteries and cause heart attacks, than U.S. residents do.

Two Sides to the Story

A study published in the January 9, 2003, issue of *The New England Journal of Medicine* found that moderate alcohol consumption by adult males may be beneficial to their health. The article, "Roles of Drinking Pattern and Type of Alcohol Consumed in Coronary Heart Disease in Men," reported on a twelve-year study of 38,077 men. It concluded that it was the frequency of drinking—not the amount, the type of alcohol, or whether or not it was consumed with a meal—that was the key factor in lowering the risk of heart disease. Men who consumed no less—and no more!—than two drinks a day three or four days a week had 68 percent less risk of having a heart attack than men who drank alcohol less than once a week. *The New*

LUNCHING AT A BISTRO IN PARIS, FRANCE, THESE TWO MEN ENJOY WINE WITH THEIR MEAL. IT IS COMMON IN COUNTRIES LIKE FRANCE, ITALY, AND SPAIN FOR WINE TO ROUTINELY BE THE BEVERAGE OF CHOICE. IN MODERATION, IT MAY EVEN HAVE BENEFICIAL HEALTH EFFECTS ACCORDING TO RECENT STUDIES.

York Times reported that a study of 80,000 American women showed that ". . . those who drank moderately had only half the heart attack risk of those who did not drink at all, even if they were slim, did not smoke, and exercised daily." The director of the National Institute on Alcohol Abuse and Alcoholism, Dr. Li, observed that recent studies confirmed previous evidence of "a strong association between light-to-moderate alcohol consumption and reduced risk of heart disease."

Other studies of Dutch, German, and Norwegian beer drinkers, of Japanese wine drinkers, and of American drinkers of hard liquor confirmed that "alcohol is beneficial in all three beverages," according to Dr. Eric Rimm, an associate professor at the Harvard School of Public Health. He adds that to stave off heart disease, small quantities of alcohol should be taken regularly—a glass with the evening meal rather than half a dozen glasses on Saturday night.

Minimizing the risk of heart attacks is not the only benefit of regular moderate drinking for adults. A recently published study from the Netherlands found that moderate drinkers over age fifty-five had a lower risk of developing dementia than non-drinkers. There is also evidence that moderate drinking may help prevent strokes and some varieties of cancer. In women, however, there is a link between alcohol and breast cancer, as well as dangers associated with pregnancy.

Bottom Line on Bottoms Up

Studies have revealed that drinking alcohol can be both beneficial and harmful. Some highlights:

DRINK UP . . .

• Growing evidence suggests that moderate drinking, defined as one to two drinks a day, can reduce the risk of heart disease, cancer, stroke, and dementia.

• Much has been made of the role of antioxidants, substances that help rid the body of harmful materials. Though red wine has gotten much of the buzz as a source of antioxidants, white wine, beer, and even hard liquor have been linked to raising antioxidant levels in the blood.

• Some studies found benefits only among certain groups. One recent study found alcohol helps ward off heart disease for women forty and older, but not men. Another study found alcohol helped middle-aged drinkers of both genders.

. . . BUT KNOW THIS

• Damage wrought by heavy drinking outweighs any benefit. It can damage the esophagus, stomach, intestines, liver, and pancreas. Alcohol abuse can also contribute to increased breast-cancer risk in some women.

• A warning about taking aspirin with alcohol: The combination irritates the stomach lining.

• The American Medical Association has found that young adult drinkers risk long-term brain damage, especially in learning, memory, and critical thinking.

• The American Heart Association does not advise people to drink to attain the touted health effects. But many may not want to hear its preferred prescription: plenty of exercise, lots of vegetables, and forget the cigarettes.

—From Newsday, Jan. 9, 2003

It is important to remember that the studies demonstrating benefits of alcohol are all of adults. The subjects' bodies, brains, and emotional systems were fully developed. It can be a very different story for young people. According to Dr. Arthur Klatsky, a senior consultant in cardiology at the Kaiser-Permanente Medical Center, teenagers have a negligible risk of heart disease and for them the risks of heavy drinking vastly outweigh any benefits of moderate drinking. In one recent survey, young adults who reported drinking three to five drinks a day had death rates twice as high as nondrinkers. The dangers should be considered carefully when making decisions about drinking.

THE TEMPERANCE CRUSADE—WHO WILL WIN?

IN THE FACE OF SNEERING MALE ALCOHOL DRINKERS, NINETEENTH CENTURY WOMEN TEMPERANCE CRUSADERS TRY TO PRAY THEM AWAY FROM THEIR ADDICTION TO LIQUOR. THESE WOMEN WERE RIDICULED, AND EVEN TODAY ARE REGARDED SKEPTICALLY, BUT THEY HAD GOOD REASON FOR PURSUING THEIR CAUSE FERVENTLY. IT WAS COMMON FOR MANY WORKING CLASS MEN TO DRINK UP THEIR PAYCHECKS WITHOUT REGARD TO THEIR FAMILY'S NEEDS, AND LIQUOR-CAUSED WIFE AND CHILD ABUSE WAS ALL TOO COMMON.

2 The Noble Experiment

Both alcohol and alcoholism have been part of American history from the start. According to the *Encyclopedia of American Social History*, "Americans have long been among the world's heaviest drinkers" and "from colonial times to the present alcohol has been pervasive in American society." The very first Dutch and English settlers drank both beer and gin and traded spirits to native Americans in exchange for land and furs, meat and produce.

Tavern and Hearth

In the seventeenth century gin was a newly con-cocted liquor, the invention of Franciscus Sylvius, a professor of medicine of the University of Leiden, in

Holland. His aim had been to create a cheap medicine combining alcohol with juniper berries. Called *jenever* in Dutch, it soon became more popular as a beverage than as a medicine. During a war between England and the Netherlands, British soldiers got in the habit of drinking it before battle and gave it the nickname "Dutch courage." They shortened the name to gin and brought it back to England when they returned from the wars. Here, because it was cheap to make and readily available, it became as popular as beer, particularly among poor people.

Gin was a favorite tavern drink in the New World under the reign of both the Dutch and the English. A few words from an otherwise forgotten tavern song capture the spirit of its popularity. "For it's gin, gin, gin/that make you want to sin" went the refrain. Indeed, the New World taverns were often brothels as well.

Except for prostitutes, taverns were men-only establishments. However, settlers of both sexes and all ages drank beer with their meals at home. Since imported beer was expensive, they brewed their own, known as small beer, which contained about one percent alcohol. Housewives brewed small beer once or twice a week. But because it was weak, by the 1700s most Americans had switched to a home brew of hard apple cider with a 6 percent to 12 percent alcohol content. This was drunk in large quantities with meals. President John Adams consumed a quart of hard apple cider a day and lived to be ninety years old.

The slave trade introduced rum, as well as molasses, to the colonies. Soon rum was as popular as gin in the taverns. Enterprising businessmen built distilleries in New England and manufactured rum from molasses. This could be sold more cheaply than imported rum, and its sweetness, as opposed to other liquors' harshness, made it increasingly popular.

The Temperance Movement Is Born

Some people drank, and some people objected to drinking. New England Puritans considered alcohol the "Good Creature of God" that promoted digestion, improved health, and increased strength. However, they deplored drunkenness and came to be concerned that alcohol caused fights, family discord, and crime. They licensed taverns, and only upstanding and moral men and women of the community were granted licenses. Some Puritan towns nailed up lists of names of citizens banned from buying liquor. Ministers kept track of how long drinkers stayed in taverns.

During the American Revolution an English blockade cut off the supply of molasses used to make rum. In the South, Scotch-Irish immigrants began distilling whiskey from a combination of corn, wheat, and rye. The result was bourbon. It was considered patriotic to drink it rather than imported spirits. At the same time, opposition to hard liquor began to build. Quakers blamed alcohol for business failures, and Methodists condemned drinking alcohol as immoral. Benjamin Rush, a Philadelphia physician, published *An Inquiry into the Effects of Spirituous Liquors* in 1784. The tract presented evidence that hard drinking could ruin a person's health. Its publication marked the beginning of the temperance movement—the campaign to ban liquor—in the United States.

There was a lot of whiskey produced in America at this time. It was very cheap: a fifth of a gallon sold for five cents. Beer and wine were more expensive, and so were drunk mostly by the more well-to-do. Also, water was often contaminated, and in the short run whiskey was safer to drink. By the early 1800s Americans were consuming roughly seven gallons of 100 percent alcohol per adult per year.

A Teetotal Victory

As the national thirst grew, so did the temperance movement. "Demon Rum" was denounced from the pulpits of many denominations. New England Congregationalists told their flocks that liquor was bad for their souls and that it was the work of the devil. In the 1830s Evangelical Protestants began a campaign to convert drinkers into teetotalers. They brought pressure on the wealthy to renounce wine and on farmers to destroy apple orchards in order to do away with hard cider.

Back then the United States was mostly a small-town society. Neighbors' opinions counted. Social

THE DEMONS IN THE DISTILLERY. (COPIED FROM A CUT IN THE PAMPHLET.)

A TEMPERANCE PAMPHLET PUBLISHED IN SALEM, MASSACHUSETTS IN THE 1830S PORTRAYS THE DEMONS OF RUM WORKING IN THE NETHER REGIONS OF HELL TO DESTROY ALL THAT IS DECENT AND HOLY BY MAKING AND DISTRIBUTING ALCOHOL.

and religious pressure made many people give up the bottle. The early temperance campaign was remarkably successful. Between 1825 and 1840 alcohol consumption declined by about half. Nearly half the nation's population no longer drank alcohol. The other half, however, kept on guzzling.

In the 1840s and 1850s large numbers of Irish and German immigrants arrived. Beer and whiskey were part of their cultures. In the cities, and later in the small towns, Irish bars and German beer gardens sprang up. The Irish were Catholic, as were many of the Germans. The temperance movement was composed mostly of Protestants. Soon religious prejudice became part of the battles.

Maine banned alcohol and became the first so-called dry state, in 1851. However, the law proved difficult to enforce and was soon repealed. Many small communities—728 of 856 towns in New York State, for instance—also voted themselves dry only to repeal their antiliquor laws.

The Women's Christian Temperance Union (WCTU)

Whiskey, still the most inexpensive alcoholic beverage, was a major problem in the ranks of the Union Army during the Civil War. In an effort to curb the drunkenness of whiskey-drinking troops, the military authorities banned whiskey from army camps and substituted beer. Heavy alcohol taxes were imposed on whiskey, lighter taxes on beer. By the end of the war, beer was by far cheaper to drink and more plentiful. Along with the wines favored by immigrants from southern Europe, it became the drink of choice among working people and their families. Saloons, where a growler (small bucket, or pail) of beer cost a nickel and free-lunch counters offered a variety of snacks, opened in cities and towns across America. The snacks were salty, and the more one ate, the more one drank.

The 1870s brought the beginning of America's

second major campaign against drink. In 1873 in Ohio, the Women's Temperance Crusade began sitting in at saloons and praying loudly until they closed. As the crusade spread both nationally and internationally, the Woman's Christian Temperance Union (WCTU) was born. It would become the largest women's organization in the world, with millions of members.

Different factors contributed to the success of the WCTU. Protestant denominations—particularly the Methodist church, which had close ties to the WCTU—blamed crime and a general lowering of moral standards on drinking by the foreign-born, who were mainly Roman Catholic. The WCTU was also supported by followers of Native American politicians because they thought—often correctly—that saloons were the gathering places of immigrant groups seeking to wrest political power from them. Many labor organizers were antialcohol because of the drinking patterns in company towns, where the railroad, or the coal mining company, or the factory owned the liquor stores and saloons and granted credit to buy liquor. This kept the workers in debt to their employers, prevented them from seeking jobs elsewhere, and hindered organizing by unions.

Although those who established the WCTU had come from the upper and middle classes, the greatest support eventually came from the wives of working men. Along with their children, they were the major victims of liquor. It was their husbands who charged drinks at the company saloon after a grueling ten- or twelve-hour workday. The cost was deducted from their paychecks, often leaving little left over for the women to buy necessities like food and clothing. Drunken husbands, beaten down by hard work and the lack of prospects to improve their situation, often took out their frustrations on their wives and children. Battered wives were commonplace in company towns. A pattern was established where brutalized sons grew to manhood to brutalize their wives, and daughters grew up to marry men as driven by drink as their fathers. It was easy to poke fun at the WCTU, but the reality was that strong drink had a stranglehold on lower-class society in America during the nineteenth century.

Carry Nation

A frequent target of ridicule was a zealous anti-liquor reformer named Carry Nation. Born Carry Amelia Moore on November 25, 1846, she was the daughter of a Kentucky slaveholder and a psychotic mother who spent the last three years of her life in the Missouri State Hospital for the Insane. On November 21, 1867, Carry married Dr. Charles Gloyd, a hard-drinking Union army veteran of the Civil War. Carry tried to curb his drinking in vain. Dr. Gloyd was a Mason, and to escape his wife's pleadings, he would simply go to his lodge to drink. Carry developed a strong contempt for all fraternal orders.

THE FORMIDABLE ANTI-LIQUOR CRUSADER CARRY NATION WAS A FAVORITE
SUBJECT FOR CARTOONISTS WHO OPPOSED LAWS PROHIBITING THE SALE OF
LIQUOR. THEY WERE LESS THAN KIND IN THEIR DEPICTIONS. NATION INSPIRED
FEAR IN SOME OF THE BARTENDERS WHO FOUND THEMSELVES IN HER HATCHET-
WIELDING PATH.

Hatchet Woman

"MEN, I HAVE COME TO SAVE YOU FROM A DRUNKARD'S FATE!" CARRY NATION WOULD PROCLAIM JUST BEFORE SWINGING HER HATCHET AT BOTTLES OF LIQUOR AND BARROOM FURNITURE. AGE DID NOT DETER CARRY FROM HER ANTI-LIQUOR CRUSADE. SHE KEPT AT IT RIGHT UP UNTIL HER DEATH IN 1911, THE YEAR THIS PICTURE WAS TAKEN.

On June 5, 1900, when she was fifty-three years old, Carry Nation drove her buggy to Kiowa, Kansas. Nearly 6 feet tall and 175 pounds, her arm muscles bulging—like those of a lumberjack—against the sleeves of the black-and-white dress she wore, she was an imposing figure. Early the next morning she burst through the swinging doors of a local saloon. "Men, I have come to save you from a drunkard's fate!" she announced, and proceeded to break bottles, smash kegs, and destroy the bar's mirror and front windows.

She went through the area like a tornado, destroying six saloons. Because Kansas was a dry state and saloons were illegal, she was not arrested. She was, however, finally arrested and jailed for seven weeks in Wichita, Kansas. Among the expensive saloons she had wrecked in Wichita was that of the plush Hotel Carey, where she hacked away at paneling and paintings as well as destroying beer barrels, bottles, mirrors, and glassware.

Eventually, Carry Nation, now swinging her famous hatchet, extended her axe-wielding crusade to New York, Washington, Pittsburgh, and San Francisco. Nation was arrested some thirty times, usually for "disturbing the peace." She paid her fines from her earnings as a temperance lecturer and from the sale of small souvenir hatchets, similar to those she used in her saloon wrecking crusade.

The marriage didn't last. Although pregnant, Carry left Dr. Gloyd after only a few months. He died from the effects of alcoholism six months after their child was born. To support herself and her child, as well as Dr. Gloyd's mother, Carry taught school in Holden, Missouri. In 1877 she married David Nation, a minister and lawyer nineteen years older than herself.

Carry had—or said she had—mystical experiences that filled her with a strongly expressed zeal in her crusade against liquor. After the Nation family moved to Medicine Lodge, Kansas, she helped found the local chapter of the WCTU. She led a prayer vigil in one saloon and was successful in having it closed.

Actually, the saloon had operated illegally. Kansas had adopted an amendment to the state constitution in 1880 that made it a dry state. Despite this, numerous establishments sold liquor openly. Carry Nation decided that since saloons were illegal, it was justifiable to force her way into such places and destroy not only the liquor but the furniture and fixtures as well. Saloon property, she declared, "has no rights that anybody is bound to respect."

Over the years Carry Nation's war on alcohol spread with increasing violence. Although she was regarded as a leader of the temperance movement, many of those in it deplored Nation's tactics and regarded her as an embarrassment. When she spoke on the evils of drink at college campuses like Harvard and Yale, she was often mocked by the students and hooted down. Nevertheless, despite her public image as a hatchet-swinging fanatic, Carry Nation drew attention to the temperance movement, helping to make it an important political force in America. By the time of her death in 1911, there was strong support building for national prohibition of liquor. By 1913 thirty-one states had laws restricting the sale of liquor.

Prohibition: The Eighteenth Amendment

The WCTU played a leading role in the campaign for Prohibition, but it was the Anti-Saloon League (ASL) that successfully lobbied Congress to enact anti-liquor legislation. Although women were still the leading force in the campaign, it was the backing of industrialists like John D. Rockefeller, who viewed drinking by workers in terms of lowered efficiency and lost man-hours, that gave impetus to ASL efforts.

There was some opposition from working-class men, but it was not organized. Many young men were in Europe fighting World War I when Congress passed the first liquor prohibition bill, in 1917, as an emergency wartime measure to conserve grain. There was considerable resentment among soldiers when Congress followed up the measure with a constitutional amendment to ban liquor nationwide. They felt that Prohibition had been passed behind their backs while they were away fighting for their country.

"BOOZE BUSTERS" IS WHAT LAWBREAKING DRINKERS CALLED POLICE DEPARTMENT LIQUOR SQUADS LIKE THIS ONE SHOWN POSING WITH CASES OF CONFISCATED ALCOHOL AND DISTILLING EQUIPMENT DURING PROHIBITION. THE PHOTOGRAPH DATES FROM 1922 WHEN PROHIBITION WAS STILL IN ITS EARLY DAYS.

The Eighteenth Amendment, which would be known as Prohibition, was ratified by the states in 1919 and became effective in 1920. It was backed up by the Volstead Act, which passed despite a veto by President Woodrow Wilson. This act prohibited the sale of beverages containing more than 0.5 percent alcohol. Although forty-six states ultimately ratified the Eighteenth Amendment, there was considerable opposition to Prohibition from its beginnings.

Opponents of Prohibition were called wets in contrast to the drys, who supported it. In 1919, when Prohibition was already the law of the land, the New Jersey Democratic candidate for governor, Edward I. Edwards, vowed that if he was elected, he would "make New Jersey as wet as the Atlantic Ocean." Even as alcohol consumption was being curbed in the early 1920s, one historian was describing it as "a fool's errand."

Throughout the 1920s drinkers could easily find liquor, particularly in the nation's cities. There was a wide discrepancy in enforcement of Prohibition. It was 95 percent effective in rural Kansas but only 5 percent effective in New York City. There, the 15,000 saloons that closed were replaced by 32,000 so-called speakeasies, where illegal alcohol was served in teacups or soup bowls. Two hundred thousand speakeasies were in operation around the country.

A Scientist's Conclusion

"The prestige of government has undoubtedly been lowered considerably by the Prohibition law. For nothing is more destructive of respect for the government and the law of the land than passing laws which cannot be enforced. It is an open secret that the dangerous increase of crime in this country is closely connected with this."

—Professor Albert Einstein

Turf Wars, Hijackings, and Murder

During Prohibition giant bootlegging operations were organized to supply a thirsty public. Rumrunners brought in alcohol by night. The Purple Gang of Detroit took control of smuggling liquor from Canada. Infamous gangster Al Capone's henchmen supplied liquor to Chicago and much of the Midwest in vehicles disguised as diaper service delivery trucks.

Organized crime accounted for most, but not all, of the illegal liquor that flowed. Gin became popular because it was relatively easy to make at home in the bathtub. Portable stills used to distill liquor could be bought at hardware stores for six dollars. Sometimes the home brew was harsh and hard to swallow, so it was mixed with fruit juices or flavored sodas to make it more palatable. Mixed drinks were favored by women, who were not accustomed to drinking hard liquor. Some of the cocktails that originated during Prohibition—Bloody Marys, Cuba libres, and others—are still popular today.

Turf wars and violent acts committed by armed mobs selling and transporting beer and hard liquor resulted in high crime rates and killings. Public safety during the Prohibition years became a major concern. Gangs were hijacking each other's shipments. Speakeasies were being torched or otherwise attacked for not buying their wares from a particular supplier. Machine guns were rat-a-tatting on main thoroughfares, and innocent bystanders were being killed. Bribery of police by gang lords and speakeasy owners

BROOKLYN GANGSTER AL CAPONE WENT WEST TO CHICAGO TO ESTABLISH HIS MIDWESTERN MONOPOLY ON THE DISTRIBUTION OF ILLEGAL LIQUOR. CAPONE'S MEN DISPOSED OF RIVAL GANG LEADERS AND THEIR GOON SQUADS WITH RAPID-FIRE BULLETS FROM TOMMY GUNS. MOST FAMOUS OF SUCH SO-CALLED "RUBOUTS" WAS THE MASS KILLING OF COMPETING GANG MEMBERS REMEMBERED AS THE ST. VALENTINE'S DAY MASSACRE.

was widespread. Federal agents, charged with enforcing the Prohibition laws, were also on the take. The mobs were becoming powerful enough to finance political campaigns and elect crooked politicians. The loss of tax revenue formerly generated by legal liquor sales was being felt by local and state governments, and by the federal government as well. Public resentment of the liquor ban mounted, and in 1933 the Twenty-First Amendment to the Constitution was passed and Prohibition was finally repealed.

The Aftermath

Although Prohibition is considered a failure today, it did achieve its goal. It turned many citizens into law-breaking drinkers, but while it was in force it also reduced the consumption of alcohol in the United States. It's hard to say how much the drinking of alcohol decreased, since there are no records for the amounts of illegal liquor consumed. However, it is estimated that alcohol consumption decreased by as much as half during Prohibition. This is based on evidence of the decline of deaths due to cirrhosis of the liver and a decrease in the number of alcoholics admitted for treatment to hospitals and mental institutions.

After the repeal of Prohibition tight federal controls over the sale and distribution of alcohol were put in place. High taxes were imposed to raise the price of alcohol. The hours, locations, and advertising of liquor stores were restricted. Many states imposed strict licensing procedures on these stores, limiting the number of licenses to be made available. Some states banned bars and restricted drinking to bottle clubs where membership was limited and supervised. In many states wine and hard liquor could not be bought in grocery stores or supermarkets. Beer was more easily available, and beer sales have steadily gone up over the years. Hard liquor sales began to shoot up during the boom in the post-World War II economy of the 1950s. The 1960s saw a shift from bourbon to scotch. This was followed by a rise in popularity of sweet mixed drinks with rum or vodka bases, and by the 1980s and 1990s sales of premixed hard liquor products were increasing rapidly.

The most surprising shift in American drinking habits was the growth in wine sales after Prohibition ended. Between 1933 and 2003 sales of imported wines from France, Italy, Spain, and other countries skyrocketed. So did consumption of wines produced in California and New York State. Around 1940, table wines—those taken with meals, such as chardonnay, rosé, and chianti—became more and more an accepted part of American dining.

Cheap wine became the drink of choice among down-and-out alcoholics. After Prohibition was repealed, campaigns to turn drinkers into teetotalers were pretty much confined to this group. The American public, both drinkers and nondrinkers, had turned against temperance. Most people agreed with the conclusion of the *Encyclopedia of American Social History* that one lesson of Prohibition is "that whenever a product is banned, it reappears illegally in a more potent form."

PEOPLE WHO DRIVE DRUNK IN MARYLAND
PROBABLY WON'T BE DRIVING MUCH LONGER

THE NATIONAL MINIMUM DRINKING AGE ACT PASSED IN 1984 IS ENFORCED STRICTLY IN STATES LIKE MARYLAND. HERE A STATE POLICE OFFICER HOLDS UP A WARNING FOR DRUNK DRIVERS WHO CROSS THE STATE LINE. THE EFFECTIVENESS OF ENFORCEMENT IS DEMONSTRATED BY THE FALLOFF IN DRUNK DRIVING ACCIDENTS, PARTICULARLY AMONG YOUNG PEOPLE.

"If we meet with a candidate and like them, we give them $10,000 on the spot. . . . When someone commits $10,000 to you, you don't forget that."

—David K. Rehr, president of the National Beer Wholesalers Association (NBWA) describes his organization's strategy for contributing to politicians.

3 Liquor: Lobbies and Laws

Shortly before he left his quarters on that fateful November evening in 1998, twenty-nine-year-old Daniel J. Hill of Anchorage, Alaska, told his landlady he would be partying and drinking all he could because he'd soon be going to jail as the result of a drunken driving conviction in which he had run a red light and injured two people. There had also been previous convictions for drunken driving and leaving the scene of the accident. Now Hill would again be drinking and driving without a license. The Subaru he'd be driving was unregistered, unlicensed, and uninsured.

Later that night twenty-one-year-old Aric Thompson was pedaling his bicycle along the edge

IN OCTOBER 2000, PRESIDENT BILL CLINTON SIGNED INTO LAW AN IMPROVED STANDARD FOR IDENTIFYING DRUNK DRIVERS. HE IS SHOWN HERE WITH MILLIE WEBB (L.), NATIONAL PRESIDENT OF MOTHERS AGAINST DRUNK DRIVERS (MADD). MS. WEBB'S NINETEEN-MONTH-OLD NEPHEW WAS KILLED BY A DRUNK DRIVER.

of Dowling Road in Anchorage. A journalism student at the University of Alaska, Aric was a poet and guitar player. He had recently decided to seek a career in radio. Friends agreed with his mother's description of him as "a wonderful, gentle spirit."

The Subaru, with a drunken Daniel J. Hill at the wheel, came barreling down Dowling Road and swerved out of control. It struck Aric Thompson, severing one of his legs, throwing him fifteen feet into the air, and killing him. Hill and the Subaru kept on going. It was only later that police traced the car and arrested him.

Mothers Against Drink Driving (MADD)

Approximately 25,000 people are killed each year because of accidents involving drunk driving. Alcohol is a factor in four out of ten traffic deaths. Mothers Against Drunk Driving (MADD) estimates that 500,000 Americans are injured each year in alcohol-related crashes.

MADD is a national organization that began in 1980. In September of that year, twenty-year-old Joe Tursi was driving near Philadelphia when a truck with a drunk driver at the wheel crossed the centerline of the highway and hit his car head-on. The front of the truck went through his windshield and crushed his head. Joe Tursi lived on life support for almost a week before dying.

The driver of the truck was convicted of vehicular

homicide and sentenced to four years probation and a fine of $151. Outraged by such leniency toward the killer of her son, Marie Tursi established the first chapter of MADD in Pennsylvania. Today, there are chapters of MADD in forty-two counties in Pennsylvania, and hundreds more throughout the United States and Canada.

MADD was particularly active in generating support for establishing a lower national standard for blood alcohol concentration (BAC), which determines if a driver is legally drunk. The question of what level BAC defines a driver's inability to function behind the wheel was at the center of the controversy over the federal law signed by President Clinton in 2000. Prior to its passing, the BAC had been set by individual states. The alcohol industry strongly objected to establishing a low national standard.

The New BAC National Standard

The National Highway Traffic Safety Administration had determined that drivers with an 0.08 percent BAC showed significant impairment in their ability to brake, steer, and change lanes. Before the federal law was passed, only eighteen states met that standard. All other states had limits of 0.10 percent. Those who favored lowering the standard nationally to 0.08 percent believed it would have a significant effect in reducing highway carnage.

POLICE OFFICER ADMINISTERS A "WALK-THE-STRAIGHT-LINE" SOBRIETY TEST TO
A YOUTH HE SUSPECTS OF DRIVING WHILE INTOXICATED. THIS IS ONLY A FIRST
STEP IN DETERMINING INEBRIATION. THE CLINCHER IS THE TEST TO MEASURE THE
BLOOD ALCOHOL CONTENT (BAC) LEVEL. A LEVEL OF .08 PERCENT HAS BEEN
FOUND TO IMPAIR STEERING, BRAKING, AND LANE CHANGING JUDGMENT.

Under the new law, a state that fails to comply with the national standard loses 2 percent of its federal highway funds starting in 2004. The penalty increases to 4 percent in 2005, 6 percent in 2006, and 8 percent in 2007. Objections have been raised to the federal government's withholding of highway funds for noncompliance, on the grounds that it is coercive and possibly unconstitutional.

In opposing the law, the National Beer Wholesalers Association points out that the Twenty-First Amendment gives states the right to regulate alcoholic beverages. Standards, opponents claim, should be different for areas of the country with population densities as dissimilar— for example—as Manhattan and Wyoming. The Distilled Spirits Council of the United States (DISCUS) agrees that the BAC standard is "a state issue and should be decided by each state." Other representatives of the liquor industry argue that stricter BAC rules only intimidate social drinkers while having no effect on alcoholics and habitual drunk drivers.

BAC standards are one of four ongoing issues subject to state and federal legislation that concern the alcohol industry. The others are the raising of taxes, limitations on liquor industry advertising, government-financed antialcohol advertising, and lowering the national legal drinking age from twenty-one to eighteen. Taking strong stands on these issues, the alcohol industry between 1997 and 1999 spent $21.9 million on lobbying federal lawmakers. According to George A. Hacker, director of alcohol policies for the Center for Science in the Public Interest, "legislation has been deferred or defeated, issues have been forgotten or deep-sixed for the convenience of alcohol contributors."

Taxing Liquor: Pro and Con

High taxes on alcohol, known as sin taxes, have been a traditional means of raising money for governments. The first United States Secretary of the Treasury, Alexander Hamilton, convinced Congress to tax liquor to pay off Revolutionary War debts that the government had assumed from the Colonies. This sparked the 1794 Whiskey Rebellion by small farmers who converted their surplus grain into whiskey that could be easily transported and sold. They attacked federal tax collectors and burned down the home of the regional tax inspector in Pennsylvania. As the rebellion grew, President Washington dispatched 13,000 troops to put it down.

Eighty years later, in 1875, a group of U.S. distillers formed the Whiskey Ring with the purpose of avoiding federal liquor taxes. They bribed Internal Revenue officials and tax collectors. When the conspiracy was uncovered, there were allegations that the withheld tax money would be used to finance the reelection of President Ulysses S. Grant. These were never proved, but there were

238 indictments and 110 convictions of Whiskey Ring conspirators.

Since that time taxes from the sale of liquor have been an effective source of revenue for both the federal government and the individual states. An advocate for raising liquor taxes, Cornell University associate professor Donald S. Kenkel writes that there is strong evidence that "when alcohol taxes go up, heavy drinking, drunk driving, cirrhosis and traffic fatalities fall." He estimates that an alcohol tax increase of 10 percent would lead to a 5 percent to 10 percent decrease in heavy drinking. Other high-liquor-tax advocates point out that young people, who are the biggest customers for beer and pre-mixed liquor, are most likely to drink less when what they drink costs more.

Brown University professor of anthropology Dwight B. Heath disagrees. He believes that a tax on alcohol might reduce purchases by moderate drinkers, but that it would not cause problem drinkers, who are more prone to accidents and crime, to cut back. It would make no sense, he points out, "to adopt a policy that would deny moderate drinkers the cardiovascular health benefits" of moderate drinking. David K. Rehr, president of the NBWA, puts it more bluntly. "Tax dollars," he said, "shouldn't be used to put out of business a legal product."

The Advertising Controversy
The same argument has been used by the alcohol industry when fighting attempts by MADD and

other concerned groups to obtain federal funding for an antialcohol advertising campaign. In 1999 a House of Representatives subcommittee voted to authorize the Office of National Drug Control Policy to use some of its $18 billion annual budget for anti-liquor ads that target underage drinking. Responding to the alcohol lobby, Representative Anne Northup of Kentucky led the fight against the measure. During the previous six years Ms. Northup had received donations of over $57,800 from alcohol-related political action committees (PACs). The House Appropriations Committee voted down the measure to fund antialcohol ads. A similar proposal sponsored in the Senate by New Jersey senator Frank Lautenberg was voted down in the Senate by a 54 to 43 vote.

Those who favor such measures see them as necessary to combat the large amounts of money spent on wine and beer advertising on television. The beer industry alone spends $600 million a year on TV commercials. Many of these are slotted into such high-profile sports events as the Super Bowl and the World Series, which are widely watched by young male adults. The ads often feature attractive, provocatively dressed young women, the message being that guys drinking the particular brand of beer advertised will attract them. TV ads containing subliminal sex messages—commercials with an underlying implication that young beer drinkers get the most desirable women—have become more and more common.

Rules for Advertising

In order to demonstrate a responsible attitude toward the public, the alcohol industry has devised some rules for advertising, sales, and distribution of its product. Following are excerpts from the DISCUS Code of Advertising.

• Distilled spirits should not be advertised or marketed in any manner directed or primarily intended to appeal to persons below the legal purchase age.

• Distilled spirits advertising and marketing should not be placed in any communication intended to appeal primarily to individuals below the legal purchase age.

• Distilled spirits should not be advertised on college and university campuses or in college and university newspapers.

• Distilled spirits advertising and marketing should not be specifically aimed at events where most of the audience is reasonably expected to be below the legal purchase age.

• Distilled spirits advertising should not be placed on any outdoor stationary location within 500 feet of an established place of worship or an elementary school or secondary school except on a licensed premise.

• The content of distilled spirits advertising and marketing materials should not be intended to appeal primarily to individuals below the legal purchase age.

• Distilled spirits advertising and marketing materials should contain no claims or representations that individuals can obtain social, professional, educational, or athletic success or status as a result of beverage alcohol consumption.

• Distilled spirits advertising and marketing materials should not portray, encourage, or condone drunk driving.

• No distilled spirits advertising or marketing materials should claim or depict sexual prowess as a result of beverage alcohol consumption.

—Source: Distilled Spirits Council of the United States, Inc. (DISCUS)

The entire alcohol industry opposed shifting federal funding from antidrug advertising to anti-liquor advertising. They also fought back in another way. Up to this time, makers of distilled spirits—hard liquor—had not advertised on TV. In 1995 DISCUS decided to end its voluntary ban on placing hard liquor ads on television. Seagram & Sons aired a whiskey ad on a Texas TV station in June of that year. But all of the major TV networks decided to reject hard liquor ads, and the alcohol industry had to back off.

In fairness it should be noted that DISCUS, unlike the beer industry, has a strict code regarding ads for liquor. The recommendations are enforced by a five-member Code Review Board selected from the board of directors of DISCUS. Member companies of DISCUS have been part of efforts to combat drunk driving and underage drinking. DISCUS has supported national campaigns such as "Friends Don't Let Friends Drive Drunk."

The National Minimum Drinking Age Act

The most relevant liquor-related issue for young people is the minimum legal drinking age (MLDA). The federal law covering it is the National Minimum Drinking Age Act of 1984, which established an MLDA of twenty-one throughout the country. Federal highway funds would be withheld from states that did not comply. Although all states were in compliance by 1987, the law had—and continues to have—loopholes that allow some underage individuals to legally drink.

As of March 2002, nineteen states made exceptions to the under-twenty-one drinking ban. These included the legal sale of liquor to a minor when accompanied by an adult spouse, a parent, or legal guardian. Other exceptions are made for minors purchasing wine for religious purposes or alcohol for medical purposes. In some states, minors can buy liquor in the course of lawful employment by a licensed manufacturer. In others, they may drink in private clubs.

Since its passage the National Minimum Drinking Age Act has remained controversial. Those who support it, like the National Council on Alcoholism and Drug Dependence, point out that before the act was passed, underage drivers would cross borders to buy liquor in states where the age limits were lower and then drive back while under the influence of alcohol. After the law was passed, bars and other sellers of alcohol did not want to risk federal penalties by selling to minors across state lines. Young people came to realize that they could not drive to other states for liquor, and traffic fatalities decreased. According to the National Highway Traffic Safety Administration (NHTSA), after the minimum age was standardized at twenty-one, annual traffic fatalities for underage drivers dropped by 43 percent (from 5,062 alcohol-related fatalities to 2,883) between 1987 and 1996. Other advocates of the law believe that reducing underage drinking will in turn reduce teen suicides, adolescent venereal disease, vandalism, violence in the schools, and street crime.

Opponents say there is no hard evidence that this is so. They point out that there has been a reduction of drunk driving fatalities among the general population, not just underage drinkers. They point to statistics showing that college binge drinking has not declined. They contend that under-twenty-one laws are easily circumvented with false IDs, that in any case most bars and stores that sell beer and other alcohol do not check IDs, and that a twenty-one-year-old will often do the buying for a group of younger friends.

A Tough Question

In 1996 Representative Scott Klug of Wisconsin introduced a bill called the States Rights Act that would have stopped the federal government from withholding highway funds to states that did not comply with the over-twenty-one MLDA. The bill never got out of committee. Nevertheless, it reflected an attitude by opponents that it was unfair to allow eighteen- to twenty-year-olds to marry; have children; own cars, homes, and even firearms;

and still forbid them to drink. Seen as unfair by many people is the fact that the government encourages eighteen-year olds to fight for their country but denies them a glass of beer.

Often, communication over alcohol problems is not easy for mothers and daughters. An adolescent who drinks is often in denial when it comes to admitting that she has a problem. A concerned parent, frustrated by an inability to get the young person to discuss her drinking, should seriously consider seeking outside help.

4 A Problem in the Family

Information provided by the National Clearing-house for Alcohol and Drug Information indicates that there are over 3 million teenage alcoholics in the United States today. Several million more may have serious drinking problems that they cannot handle without help. National surveys indicate that approximately one-third of high school seniors and 42 percent of college students engage in binge drinking. Underage drinkers consume about 25 percent of all alcoholic beverages in the United States.

Young adults' dependence on alcohol is a contributing factor to depression, anxiety, and antisocial behavior. Liquor plays a leading role in car crashes, suicides, and murders—the three leading causes of death for fifteen- to twenty-four-year-olds. Overeating, which leads to obesity (the number one health problem for teenagers in the nation today), often occurs when high-fat meals are washed down with alcoholic drinks that lower one's ability to push away from the table. Food makes one thirsty. Liquor can make one hungry and impair judgment. Overeating and alcoholism can combine to create a vicious, self-destructive cycle.

The Greater Danger: Alcohol, Not Drugs!

• The overall financial cost of alcohol abuse to society is 50 percent more than that of illicit drug abuse.

• Alcohol-related deaths outnumber illicit drug-related deaths by four to one.

• In 1999 the federal government spent $18 billion on illicit-drug programs and less than $1 billion on alcohol-specific programs.

—*Source: Common Sense: Drug Strategies*

The Heredity Theory

On average, young people first try alcohol at twelve years of age. Even by the most permissive standards, that is too young to handle alcohol. Nevertheless, while the risks are real, not every young drinker is going to end up an alcoholic or beset by alcohol abuse problems. Why then do some young people drink and go on with their lives in a normal fashion, while others become addicted to alcohol and are afflicted by the problems that accompany this condition?

There have been many theories explaining this phenomenon. One of the most widely accepted has to do with genes. Genetic theory—the study of genes—is complicated. For the purposes of this discussion, it's enough to know that genes are the element of the body's chemistry that passes down traits from parents to children. Among these traits are the way one looks (a small nose, big ears), the particular diseases one is most susceptible to (heart trouble, cancer, etc.), and one's behavior (a propensity toward violence, to be suicidal, or to overindulge in alcohol or drugs).

Alcoholism has long been regarded as a family trait. Recent studies suggest that there is a gene—or a combination of genes—passed on from one generation of a family to the next, that increases the possibility of a child becoming an alcoholic. According to the *Columbia University College of Physicians & Surgeons Complete Home Medical Guide*, "growing evidence supports the theory that heredity predisposes

Are You an Alcoholic?

A Simple Twelve-Question Quiz Designed to Help You Decide

1. Do you drink because you have problems? To face up to stressful situations?

2. Do you drink when you get mad at other people, your friends or parents?

3. Do you prefer to drink alone rather than with others?

4. Are you starting to get low marks? Are you goofing off at work?

5. Do you ever try to stop drinking or to drink less—and fail?

6. Have you begun to drink in the morning, before school or work?

7. Do you gulp your drinks as if to satisfy a great thirst?

8. Do you ever have loss of memory due to your drinking?

9. Do you lie about your drinking?

10. Do you ever get into trouble when you are drinking?

11. Do you often get drunk when you drink, even when you do not mean to?

12. Do you think it's cool to be able to hold your liquor?

If you can answer yes to any of these questions, maybe it's time you took a serious look at what your drinking might be doing to you.

—*Source: Alcoholics Anonymous*

some people toward alcoholism." The medical guide states that "a child of an alcoholic has four times the risk of becoming an alcoholic compared with a child of nonalcoholic parents." It further asserts that "acceptance of this condition as a disease clears the way for understanding, treatment, and recovery," but is careful to point out that "at the same time alcoholics can and must take responsibility for their own recovery."

It should also be noted that while acceptance of a genetic cause of alcoholism has been growing, the realization that it is only a theory—that as yet the studies are inconclusive—has not grown with it. There may be comfort in the idea that alcoholism is an inherited disease, because diseases are treatable. Society doesn't blame the victims of diseases. There is sympathy for diabetics and the asthmatics, whose conditions may have been passed down to them from forebears. Why should not the same attitude be applied to alcoholics? One answer by critics of the genetic theory is that it tends to relieve alcoholics of responsibility for their condition while at the same time reinforcing the notion that curing it is hopeless.

Help Is Available

Alcoholism researcher George E. Vaillant, author of *The Natural History of Alcoholism Revisited*, believes that "the high number of children of alcoholics who become addicted is due less to biological factors than to poor role models." A growing number of experts have come to believe that alcoholics are neither born nor become alcoholics with their first drink. Rather, they see a progression over a period of time that evolves from occasional drinking to steady drinking to problem drinking to alcoholism. Although the progression is not inevitable, it should be stressed that there is considerable evidence that those who begin drinking before age fifteen are four times as likely to become alcoholics as those who start at age twenty-one or twenty-two.

The course for the younger group, however, is not irreversible. Young adults who find themselves trapped in an alcoholic drinking pattern can rescue themselves. The first step is recognizing that there is a problem. (The sidebar quiz can help do that.) Acknowledging that help is available is the next step, and actively seeking that help, the one after that.

Ideally, parents are the ones to whom the young drinker should turn for help. Practically, for any number of reasons, alcoholic youth may be reluctant to disclose drinking problems to their parents. A school guidance counselor or social worker may be less judgmental or—because they have less emotional involvement—have a clearer perspective of the problem. Talking things over with a counselor may not cure the problem drinker, but it will help to point him or her in the direction of more active and ongoing help. Many schools have Student Assistance Programs (SAPs) designed to identify, assess, refer, and support students with alcohol problems.

Referrals from counselors and SAPs will vary from place to place. There are an abundance of options available to help young people with drinking problems. Among them are:

• scheduled meetings with school guidance counselors or social workers trained to help assess a student's use of alcohol;

• group therapy programs in which young drinkers meet for two hours after school every day, and their families meet twice a week with other families coping with the same problem;

• participation in local chapters of Alcoholics Anonymous or some similar organization, and interaction with an organization sponsor who has been sober for at least three years;

• rehabs that offer live-in rehabilitation programs for two to twelve weeks;

• therapeutic communities in which young people live for up to two years in order to overcome their addiction and related problems.

Children of Alcoholics (COAs)

Young adults who rarely or never drink may still have alcoholism issues in the person of a mother or father who is a problem drinker. According to Sarah Hines Martin—who grew up with an alcoholic father and who now counsels children of problem drinkers in Atlanta—in an average classroom six students will have a parent who drinks to excess. The National Association for Children of Alcoholics estimates that there are 26.8 million children of alcoholics (COAs) in the United States today and that over 11 million are under the age of eighteen. Other sources place the number of minor COAs at as high as 20 million.

A natural first reaction to realizing that Mom or Dad drinks too much is denial. Another common reaction is for offspring to blame themselves for their parent's drinking. If they had only cleaned their room, done the dishes—whatever—then Ma wouldn't have to hit the bottle. If they had come home on time, hadn't talked back—et cetera—then Pop wouldn't hang out in the bar.

This is nonsense. The daughter or son is not to blame. It is most important that the children of alcoholics understand this and accept it. There may be a whole lot o' reasons why parents drink, but their children are not the basic cause. No matter how hard an offspring tries, he or she can't stop a parent from drinking. The child didn't cause his or her parent's alcoholism, and the child can't cure it. The parent is an adult, and if there are issues with his or her child, they should be addressed, not drowned in alcohol.

It may seem harsh, but the son or daughter may have to be selfish. There is often a temptation to deal with alcoholic parents by outdrinking them. It's a way of becoming a part of their world, of validating their role as parents by emulating them, but it doesn't work. Becoming a drunk doesn't help them. It only carries on a self-destructive pattern that will ruin their child's life along with their own.

Some Dos and Don'ts

What can a young adult do if he or she lives in a house where one or both parents are loving sometimes and falling-down drunk other times. What if a drunken parent gets violent? What if the other parent or the child is the victim? What if the young person finds himself or herself in a car being driven erratically by a parent who has had one too many?

For starters, he should find an adult he can trust and discuss the problem with that person. If there is no family member available, he might talk to a teacher, a doctor, a member of the clergy, or a school counselor. If there is nobody he feels comfortable with, he may contact Alateen, a help-group that deals specifically with the problems of children with alcoholic parents. (They may need to call Al-Anon or Alcoholics Anonymous to locate Alateen in their area.)

A young adult in this situation should try not to make his or her parent's drinking the focus of her life. She should make an effort to involve herself in other activities—team sports, the chess club, a drama group, whatever. She should never be ashamed and should not withdraw from friends. True friends can help with the support she needs. They may be surprised to find that one of them is trying to cope with the same problem that she is.

Children of parents who drink should not try to hide their parent's alcohol. They should not pour it down the sink. Doing so might make the drinker angry, and it won't solve the problem. It only sets up a contest that the parent inevitably wins by getting another bottle and continuing to drink. If the son or daughter wins the contest, the victory will only be temporary, and it might lead to violence.

Siblings and Friends

If a drunken parent becomes violent toward his or her child or some other family member, the young person should not try to deal with it directly. Violent alcoholics rarely respond to reason. Confrontation only makes them more violent. This is the time when the youngster must be very strong. He or she should go to an adult neighbor for help or get out of the house and call the police. It is a terrible feeling to have to call the police to deal with a violent parent, but it is much worse if the violence isn't stopped and it becomes necessary to deal with the results of it. The young person who doesn't act to get help may well become the victim of violence again.

If a parent is not violent but drives when drunk and often insists a child ride with him or her, the off-spring might want to contact Us Kids, an organization of young adults who deal with this problem. They point out that if a parent drives while drunk with a minor in the car, he or she is guilty of violating the Child Endangerment Law. They are working to have the law changed so that driving drunk with an underage passenger can be prosecuted as child abuse. Even children who don't want to be in the position of involving a parent with the law may find it helpful to contact Us Kids just to talk to others dealing with parents who drive while intoxicated.

Techniques for dealing with siblings who drink are pretty much the same as those for dealing with alcoholic parents. They are, however, complicated by the relationship between older and younger brothers and sisters. Older siblings may simply brush off the concerns of a younger brother or sister. Younger siblings might resent advice that resembles parental authority. Each case will be different, depending on the individual relationship. The overall recommendation is to tread very lightly.

This is also valid advice when dealing with friends who have drinking problems. A person may want to help them, but doesn't want to alienate them. If a friend points out that their buddy has a drinking problem, he or she may deny it. However, if she has admitted that she has a drinking problem, she may be willing to talk about it. If she is engaging in other self-destructive behaviors—drugs, shoplifting, unprotected sex—related to her drinking, the peer in whom she has confided may be faced with the question of whether or not to tell an adult about it. If she is binge drinking, an adult should intervene. But bringing in an adult means betraying a friend, perhaps betraying a confidence. It's a hard call. Nevertheless, where suicide or behavior so dangerous as to threaten death is concerned, a true friend has no choice but to act. He or she may lose a friend but will save a life.

God, grant me the Serenity
To accept the things I cannot change . . .
Courage to change the things I can,
And Wisdom to know the difference.

—"The Serenity Prayer" by Dr. Reinhold Niebuhr was
integrated by Bill W., cofounder of Alcoholics
Anonymous, into the group's philosophy.

5 Help, Hope, and Healing

A drunk was a drunk, an object of disapproval, disgust, and contempt in Akron, Ohio, in 1935. That was pretty much the attitude throughout the country. However, 1935 was the year that Bill W., a stockbroker, met with Dr. Bob S., an Akron surgeon, and the program was born that would view drunks as alcoholics—and as human beings.

Both men were recovering alcoholics who had overcome their dependency on drink. Bill had concluded that alcoholism was a sickness of mind, body, and spirit, and Dr. Bob was soon convinced that he was right. Together, they initiated a program to work with alcoholics at a local hospital. Calling themselves a fellowship, they started groups in New York City and Cleveland, as well as Akron. Their work went slowly, and it took over four years before they could claim sobriety for one hundred members in the three groups. In 1939 Bill W. authored *Alcoholics Anonymous*, which spelled out their philosophy and methods, including the Twelve Steps of Recovery for alcoholics.

The book brought new members, and as word spread, the media took notice and stories began to appear with case histories of those helped by Alcoholics Anonymous (A.A.), as the movement was now called. There were—and are—no dues for A.A. membership. Anonymity is taken very seriously. People are only members of A.A. when they choose to say that they are members. The only requirement is a desire to stop drinking.

Is Alcoholics Anonymous Flawed?

A.A. estimates that its current worldwide membership at over two million with 100,000 groups in 150 countries. The membership in the United States is roughly 1,170,000. Conservatively, A.A. has helped some two million people stop drinking since its inception almost seventy years ago. Nevertheless, some people concerned with alcoholism believe that A.A. is not always effective. As far back as 1987, *U.S. News and World Report* disclosed that "outside researchers . . . believe that perhaps four out of five people who go to A.A. meetings soon drop out." In his book *Heavy Drinking*, Professor Herbert Fingarette, a former consultant to the World Health Organization, commented that "the A.A. program of recovery is simply not acceptable or attractive to the majority of people suffering problems from drinking."

The emphasis on belief in a higher power (which some people view as a religious orientation) that is stressed in the A.A. Twelve Steps turns off some who seek help from A.A.. The A.A. philosophy that alcoholism is a disease that can never be cured but only contained through constant vigilance and determined sobriety is questioned by others. The concept that people fall off the wagon because they have "not hit bottom" is regarded as a built-in excuse for continuing to drink periodically while sporadically attending A.A. meetings. The pressure to stand up and confess one's alcoholism and one's destructive behavior publicly is considered counterproductive to recruitment by some who have studied alcoholics' behavior. Finally, A.A. has come to be regarded as the linchpin of the antialcohol establishment, tied in to those organizations—government, as well as business and religious—that support its efforts. This, say critics, has resulted in a rigid approach that rejects other, nonestablishment treatment programs no matter how valid they may prove to be.

The Twelve Steps of Alcoholics Anonymous

1. We admitted we were powerless over alcohol—that our lives had become unmanageable.

2. Came to believe that a Power greater than ourselves could restore us to sanity.

3. Made a decision to turn our will and our lives over to the care of God as we understood him.

4. Made a searching and fearless moral inventory of ourselves.

5. Admitted to God, to ourselves, and to another human being the exact nature of our wrongs.

6. Were entirely ready to have God remove all these defects of character.

7. Humbly asked Him to remove our shortcomings.

8. Made a list of all persons we had harmed, and became willing to make amends to them all.

9. Made direct amends to such people wherever possible, except when to do so would injure them or others.

10. Continued to take personal inventory and when we were wrong promptly admitted it.

11. Sought through prayer and meditation to improve our conscious contact with God as we understood Him, praying only for knowledge of His will for us and the power to carry that out.

12. Having had a spiritual awakening as the result of these steps, we tried to carry this message to alcoholics, and to practice these principles in all our affairs.

Al-Anon and Alateen

Despite the criticism it receives, A.A. is still the leading organization dealing with alcoholism. It is still widely accepted as having helped many, if not all, alcoholics. Many organizations concerned with a variety of problems ranging from drug addiction to compulsive gambling and obsessive sex have patterned themselves closely on A.A.'s philosophy, methods, and program. Among the foremost spin-off movements are Al-Anon, founded in 1951, and its subsidiary, Alateen.

Although not directly affiliated with A.A., the Al-Anon program is adapted from A.A.'s Twelve Step program and concepts of service. It is designed to help anyone who is dealing with a relative's or friend's problems with alcoholism. Coping with such a situation is the only requirement for membership. Like A.A., queries and membership are kept confidential. There are over 24,000 Al-Anon groups in 115 countries.

Alateen is a branch of young Al-Anon members. Each Alateen group must have an active adult member of Al-Anon as a sponsor. Group members come together to discuss their difficulties; learn effective ways to cope with their problems; encourage one another; help each other understand the principles of the Al-Anon program; and share experience, strength, and hope with each other. Alateen members learn that compulsive drinking is a disease, that they must detach themselves emotionally from the drinker's problems while continuing to love the person, that they are not the cause of another's drinking or behavior, that they cannot change or control anyone but themselves, that they have spiritual and intellectual resources with which to develop their own potentials regardless of what happens at home, and that they can build satisfying and rewarding life experiences for themselves. There are over 2,300 Alateen groups worldwide.

A Little Bit of Medicine

Disulfiram, more commonly known by its brand name of Antabuse, is an antialcohol drug used voluntarily by chronic alcoholic patients who want to stay sober while undergoing psychological treatment for their addiction. The drug produces a sensitivity to alcohol in the body that produces extremely unpleasant reactions if the patient takes a drink. These include throbbing headaches, difficulty in breathing, heart palpitations, nausea, and vomiting. In severe cases there may be heart failure, convulsions, and even death.

Antabuse should only be used under a doctor's supervision. The patient should be made fully aware of the risks. Any substance containing alcohol—cough syrup, some salad dressings, rum cakes, and other liqueur-based desserts, for instance—must be avoided. Patients should be aware that adverse reactions may occur if alcohol is swallowed as long as fourteen days after taking Antabuse.

There is no evidence that antabuse is a cure for alcoholism. Without supportive psychotherapy it will only have a short-term effect on the hard drinker's addiction to alcohol. It should never—NEVER—be taken without the supervision of a physician.

Drinkwatchers and Women for Sobriety

Perhaps inspired by A.A., but disagreeing with them in different ways, organizations with a variety of approaches have sprung up to deal with alcoholism. One such is Drinkwatchers, founded by Ariel Winters, author of the book *Alternatives for the Problem Drinker*. Initiated as an alternative to A.A., Drinkwatchers works with behavior modification—a praise-and-reward technique that encourages limiting one's drinking based on the belief that heavy drinking is what people do rather than a symptom of what they are—and anhedonia therapy, which teaches that "the opposite of abusing anything is to treat it with respect and appreciation." According to Ms. Winters, "There are three types of people who use alcohol: the user, the abuser, and the . . . alcoholic. We are interested in helping the first two." The chronic alcoholic is referred by Drinkwatchers to detox facilities or A.A.-type treatment programs. Others are offered a choice of goals: abstinence or, when there are no medical problems involved, controlled drinking. This second goal fits in with current medical studies indicating that one or two drinks a day may have health benefits. There are presently more than fifty Drinkwatchers groups in the U.S., Canada, and Mexico.

The stated goal of Women for Sobriety (WFS) is for a member to stop drinking. A basic belief of the group is that the problems of women alcoholics are different from those of men. Historically, even after A.A. was beginning to take hold, there was a belief that women could not be alcoholics.

Fetal Alcohol Syndrome

Pregnant women who drink are in danger of causing fetal alcohol syndrome (FAS) in their unborn child. Alcohol passes into the mother's bloodstream and depresses the central nervous system of the fetus. The immature liver of the unborn child cannot effectively process the alcohol. The fetus becomes intoxicated and suffers withdrawal symptoms after the alcohol is gone.

Children born with FAS tend to be low-weight babies and to be small in stature. They may have unusual facial features including small eye openings, a flat nasal bridge, and overly short noses and/or chins. When their teeth come in, they may be misaligned or oddly shaped. They may have heart defects. Permanent damage to their central nervous system may have caused mental retardation or learning and behavior problems.

Although only a small percentage of the children born to alcoholic women suffer from FAS, there are an increasing number of FAS cases among teenagers who showed no signs of it when they were younger. Symptoms in these older children include hyperactivity, learning difficulties, and impaired judgment. Early diagnosis of FAS can help prevent these and other mental health problems. Self-destructive behavior by FAS children, even those in their teens, can be altered if the cause is recognized and the symptoms are understood. New research into FAS is pointing towards new hope for the happiness of FAS children.

When they tried to join A.A., they were often barred. Some women who were allowed in were treated quite roughly. The first alcoholic woman to join the Cleveland group was "thrown out of A.A. by the wives." As time passed, attitudes changed. But WFS continues to believe that women ·alcoholics often have gender-related problems.

The WFS program is based on positive thinking, metaphysics, meditation, group dynamics, and pursuit of health through nutrition. WFS recognizes a woman's emerging role in today's society, and her necessity for self-esteem and self-discovery. Drinking is viewed as a means to overcome stress, loneliness, frustration, and emotional deprivation related to a woman's role in what is still a male-dominated society. A New Life Acceptance Program helps members overcome the need for alcohol, stop drinking, forget the past, plan for tomorrow, and live for today.

A Jungian Approach

A very different approach to treating drinking problems is taken by the Jude Thaddeus Program of the Saint Jude Retreat House for alcoholics. Saint Jude, which is nondenominational and not affiliated with any religious group, bases its program on the research of the renowned psychiatrist Dr. Carl Jung. According to Dr. Jung, having a "vital spiritual experience" is the only way an alcoholic can recover.

This may sound close to the A.A. stress on faith, but the Jude Thaddeus program differs strongly from A.A. on one important point. Its advocates do not believe that alcoholism is a disease, and they believe that treating it as such does more harm than good to the problem drinker. Unlike A.A., they insist that relapse is not a part of the recovery process.

They view the fulfillment of a "vital spiritual experience" and the subsequent attainment of sobriety as goals best reached through a therapeutic relationship between the individual and the group in an alcohol-free environment. Individual responsibility is stressed and reinforced by shared decision-making with the Saint Jude Retreat House staff and other program participants. The Jude Thaddeus literature claims that since 1991, when the program started, 85 percent of those who follow the program have remained sober, but the claim is not confirmed by outside sources.

Targeted Groups

Many programs dealing with alcoholism target specific groups. St. Michael's House in Chicago devotes its efforts to serving the law enforcement community. It recognizes that alcoholism is a widespread problem affecting police officers and their families. Many Midwest police departments have relationships with St. Michael's House, which provides a twenty-four-hour help line to deal with the drinking problems caused by the stress and trauma of police work. There are a number of other programs around the country for members of the law enforcement community that can be easily accessed on the Internet.

Some of the programs are aimed at pregnant women who are problem drinkers. These women face the prospect of giving birth to a child suffering from fetal alcohol syndrome, a condition that puts the baby at risk of being born with brain damage and/or mental health problems. There are also programs for other subgroups, such as medical personnel, prisoners released on probation, and veterans.

Help is available from a wide variety of sources. All of them, regardless of the technique they use, have one thing in common. The person seeking treatment must genuinely want help in dealing with his or her alcohol problem. It must be stressed one more time. The first step toward recovery is to admit that one has a problem.

The central message of this new movement is not that
"alcoholism is a disease," or that "treatment works,"
but rather that permanent recovery from alcohol . . .
is not only possible but a reality in the lives of hundreds
of thousands of individuals and families.

—New Recovery Movement advocate William L. White,
author of *Slaying the Dragon: The History of
Addiction Treatment and Recovery in America*

Afterword

One of the most hopeful developments for the treatment of alcoholics is the New Recovery Movement, led by William L. White, senior research consultant at Chestnut Health Systems in Bloomington, Illinois. The New Recovery Movement stresses that a wide variety of people with drinking problems have solved their problems through a wide variety of techniques. Regarding recovery, William White writes, ". . . from individual to individual, that process may require diverse strategies and steps." Twelve Steps, controlled drinking, psychotherapy, group therapy, spiritual awakening, metaphysics, meditation, group dynamics, nutrition, antialcohol drugs such as Antabuse, and various combinations of these and other treatments have all worked for some people.

White recommends that rival organizations stop fighting with each other over the right way to treat an excessive-drinking problem and recognize that different folks require different strokes to success-fully deal with alcohol. Alcoholism caregivers must learn to tolerate differences and to be open to alter-native solutions generated by both present and for-mer alcoholics. Whether the condition is a moral problem or a medical problem, or whether it is a matter of individual self-destructiveness or society-generated pressures, is not as important as the fact that many people have overcome it.

It is important to know that there are other people out there who have come to terms with their issues with alcohol. This must be recognized by those who deal with alcoholics, by those affected by alcoholism, and by the public at large. General recognition that there are remedies for drinking compulsions will go a long way toward overcoming the hopelessness the problem drinker feels.

In the New Recovery Movement, recovered alcoholics and former problem drinkers actively reveal themselves to give hope to others. Their visi-bility will help to remove the stigma from compul-sive drinking. Persons who have drunk to excess will no longer view themselves as drunks or the lifelong

victims of an incurable disease. The New Recovery Movement may not solve the problem of alcoholism in America, but it is a sensible first step toward that goal.

Glossary

alcohol: Any beverage that contains ethanol (ethyl alcohol).

alcohol abuse: When one drinks to excess.

alcoholic: One who drinks compulsively and continually over a long period of time.

BAC: Blood alcohol concentration.

binge drinking: Drinking five alcoholic drinks or more at a single sitting.

controlled drinking: Reducing one's alcohol consumption to no more than one or two drinks a day, and maintaining that level, or reducing it.

delirium tremens (DTs): Hallucinations, sometimes paranoia, combined with loss of motor control resulting from withdrawal from excessive long-term drinking of alcohol.

distillation: The process by which an already fermented substance is heated to create a vapor which is then re-condensed into a liquor of much greater alcoholic strength.

DWI: Driving while intoxicated.

Eighteenth Amendment: The amendment to the Constitution that made the manufacture, transport, and sale of liquor illegal.

ethanol: The ethyl alcohol present in all alcoholic beverages.

fermentation: The process by which yeasts act on natural sugar and convert it to alcohol and carbon dioxide.

fetal alcohol syndrome: A variety of physical problems, including brain damage, that may have lifelong effects on the babies of mothers who drink to excess during pregnancy.

hangover: Unpleasant effects such as headache or upset stomach caused by over indulging in alcohol.

hard cider: Apple cider with a 6 to 12 percent alcohol content.

hard liquor: Term used for distilled spirits to distinguish them from fermented ones such as beer, or wine, which have less alcoholic content in terms of volume.

liquor: An alcoholic beverage made by distillation.

moderation: Defined by the American Dietetic Association as no more than one drink a day for women and no more than two drinks a day for men; standards do not apply to minors.

peer pressure: Coercion by companions to join in unwise activities such as drinking.

Prohibition: The period from 1919 to 1933 when alcoholic beverages were outlawed in the United States.

recovery: The path taken to stop drinking.

sin taxes: Levies on alcohol, tobacco, etc.

sobriety: The quality or state of being sober.

speakeasy: Illegal clubs where beer, wine, and liquor were served during Prohibition.

spirits: Distilled liquors.

Temperance movement: Nineteenth- and early twentieth-century movement to ban the sale of liquor.

Twenty-First Amendment: Constitutional amendment repealing Prohibition.

Volstead Act: The law passed by Congress that provided for the enforcement of the Eighteenth Amendment, which banned the sale of any beverage containing more than 0.5 percent alcohol.

Whiskey Ring: Nineteenth-century distillers and politicians who conspired to circumvent liquor taxes.

Woman's Christian Temperance Union (WCTU): The leading organization in the fight to ban alcoholic beverages.

Further Information

Web Sites

These organizations will provide information and help on alcohol and alcohol-related problems.

Al-Anon/Alateen
1600 Corporate Landing Parkway
Virginia Beach, VA 23454-5617
Phone: 1-888-4AL-ANON
www.al-anon.alateen.org/
E-mail: WSO@al-anon.org

Alcoholics Anonymous
475 Riverside Drive
11th Floor
New York, NY 10115
or Box 459 Grand Central Station
New York, NY 10163
www.alcoholics-anonymous.org

Alcohol Misuse Prevention Program
Amps Project
1016 Catherine Street
Ann Arbor, MI 48104-1620
Phone: 313-998-7255

Bureau of Alcohol, Tobacco and Firearms
Office of Liaison and Public Information
650 Massachusetts Ave. NW
Room 8290
Washington, DC 20226
Phone: 202-927-8500
Fax: 202-927-8868
www.atf.treas.gov
E-mail: alcohol/tobacco@atfhq.atf.treas.gov

Distilled Spirits Council of the United States (DISCUS)
Contact: Frank Coleman or Lisa Hawkins
1250 I St. NW
Suite 400
Washington, DC 20005
Phone: 202-628-3544
Fax: 202-682-8888
www.discus.org

Drinkwatchers (DW)
Contact: Ariel Winters
Box 179
Haverstraw, NY 10927
or Box 22311
San Francisco, CA 94122
Phone: 914-429-4844

Hazelden Foundation
P.O. Box 11, CO3
Center City, MN 55012-0011
Phone: 800-257-7810
www.hazelden.org
E-mail: info@hazelden.org

Mothers Against Drunk Driving (MADD)
511 E. John Carpenter Freeway
Suite 700
Irving, TX 75062
Phone: 800-438-6233
www.madd.org/home/
E-mail: info@madd.org
Victim Assistance: victims@madd.org

National Association for Children of Alcoholics (NACoA)
11426 Rockville Pike
Suite 100
Rockville, MD 20852
Phone: 888-554-2627
Fax: 301-468-0987
www.nacoa.net/coa3.htm
E-mail: nacoa@nacoa.neterols.com

National Council on Alcoholism and Drug Dependence
(NCADD)
20 Exchange Place
Suite 2902
New York, NY 10005
Phone: 212-269-7797
Fax: 212-269-7510
www.ncadd.org
E-mail: national@ncadd.org

National Institute on Alcohol Abuse and Alcoholism
(NIA.A.A)
Willco Building
6000 Executive Blvd.
Bethesda, MD 20892-7003
Phone: 301-496-4000
www.niA.A.a.nih.gov
E-mail: niA.A.aweb-r@exchange.nih.gov

New Recovery Movement
Advocates for Recovery
P.O. Box 460176
Denver, CO 80246

Phone: 303-639-9320
Fax: 303-639-9241
E-mail: afr@signalbhn.org

The Drug Education Center
1117 East Morehead Street
Charlotte, SC 28204
Phone: 704-375-3784

St. Michael's House
1759 West Adams Street
Chicago, Illinois 60612
Phone: 312-850-1099
Or 630-571-8722
Or 888-875-2470, in an emergency
www.stmichaelshouse.org/programs.htm

SMART Moves
Boys & Girls Clubs of America
1230 W. Peachtree Street NW
Atlanta, GA 30309-3494
Phone: 404-487-5700
E-mail: info@bgca.org

The Beer Institute
122 C Street NW
Suite 750
Washington, DC 20001-2150
Phone: 202-737-2337
www.beerinstitute.org
E-mail: info@beerinstitute.org

The Jude Thaddeus Program
Saint Jude Retreat House
P.O. Box 657
Hagaman, NY 12086
Phone: 888-424-2626
Or 518-842-2204
Fax: 518-842-5099
www.soberforever.net/welcome.html
E-mail: guesthouse@soberforever.org

Women For Sobriety (WFS)
P.O. Box 618
Quakertown, PA 18951-0618
Phone: 215-536-8026
www.womenforsobriety.org
E-mail: NewLife@nni.com

Books

Alagna, Magdalena. *Everything You Need to Know About the Dangers of Binge Drinking.* New York: Rosen Publishing Group, 2001.

B., Dick. *The Akron Genesis of Alcoholics Anonymous.* Kihei, HI: Paradise Research Publications, 1998.

Bellenir, Karen (Ed.). *Alcoholism Sourcebook.* Detroit, MI: Omnigraphics, 2000.

Gottfried, Ted. *Should Drugs Be Legalized?* Brookfield, CT: Twenty-First Century Books, 2000.

Hornik-Beer, Edith Lynn. *For Teenagers Living With a Parent Who Abuses Alcohol/Drugs.* Lincoln, NE: iUniverse.com, Inc., 2001.

Hyde, Margaret O., *Alcohol 101: An Overview for Teens.* Brookfield, CT: Twenty-First Century Books, 1999.

Langsen, Richard C. *When Someone in the Family Drinks Too Much.* New York: Dial Books for Young Readers, 1996.

Miner, Jane Claypool. *Alcohol and You.* Danbury, CT: Franklin Watts, 1997.

Sales, Pippa. *Alcohol Abuse: Straight Talk, Straight Answers.* Honolulu: Ixia Publications, 1999.

Siegel, Dr. Ronald K. *Intoxication: Life in Pursuit of Artificial Paradise.* New York: E. P. Dutton, 1989.

Stewart, Gail B. *Teen Alcoholics.* San Diego, CA: Lucent Books, 2000.

Trapani, Margi. *Inside a Support Group: Help for Teenage Children of Alcoholics.* New York: Rosen Publishing Group, 1997.

White, William L. *Slaying the Dragon: The History of Addiction Treatment and Recovery in America.* Bloomington, IL: Chestnut Health Systems, 1998.

Winters, Ariel. *Alternatives for the Problem Drinker.* New York: Drake Publishers, Inc., 1978.

Bibliography

In researching the subject of alcoholism, the following books were consulted:

Gottfried, Ted. *Should Drugs Be Legalized?* Brookfield, CT: Twenty-First Century Books, 2000.

Haring, Raymond V. *Shattering Myths and Mysteries of Alcohol.* Sacremento, CA: HealthSpan Communications, 1998.

Ketcham, Katherine and William F. Asbury. *Beyond the Influence: Understanding and Defeating Alcoholism.* New York: Bantam Books, 2000.

Leone, Bruno, ed. *Alcohol: Opposing Viewpoints.* San Diego, CA: Greenhaven Press, Inc., 1998.

Pluymen, Bert. *The Thinking Person's Guide to Sobriety.* New York: St. Martin's Press, 1999.

Siegel, Ronald K. *Intoxication: Life in Pursuit of Artificial Paradise.* New York: E. P. Dutton, 1989.

Stewart, Gail B. *Teen Alcoholics.* San Diego, CA: Lucent Books, 2000.

Torr, James B. (ed.). *Alcoholism: Current Controversies.* San Diego, CA: Greenhaven Press, Inc., 2000.

Vaillant, George E. *The Natural History of Alcoholism Revisited.* Cambridge, MA: Harvard University Press, 2000.

White, William L. *Slaying the Dragon: The History of Addiction Treatment and Recovery in America.* Bloomington, IL: Chestnut Health Systems, 1998.

Winters, Ariel. *Alternatives for the Problem Drinker.* New York: Drake Publishers, Inc., 1978.

Further information was obtained from the publications and Web sites of Alcoholics Anonymous; Al-Anon/Alateen; Bureau of Alcohol, Tobacco and Firearms; Distilled Spirits Council of the United

States (DISCUS); Mothers Against Drunk Driving (MADD); National Association for Children of Alcoholics (NACoA); National Council on Alcoholism and Drug Dependence (NCADD); National Institute on Alcohol Abuse and Alcoholism (NIA.A.A); Advocates for the New Recovery Movement; The Jude Thaddeus Program; and Women for Sobriety (WFS). Articles in *The New York Times, Newsday, Newsweek,* and *The Nation* also provided background and information for this book.

About the Author

TED GOTTFRIED has published over twenty books for young adults, and nonfiction, novels, articles, and short stories for adults. Among his works are a six-book series on the Holocaust, a four-book series on the rise and fall of the Soviet Union, *Should Drugs Be Legalized?* and *Open for Debate: Censorship.* He has been a publisher, editor, and critic, and has taught writing courses at New York University and Baruch College. His wife, Harriet Gottfried, has recently retired from her position as director of training and development for the New York Public Library.

Index